The **Tiny Book** of
TINY HOMES

LIVING LARGE IN SMALL SPACES

CAROLINE McKENZIE

CENTENNIAL BOOKS

The **Tiny Book** of
TINY HOMES
LIVING LARGE IN SMALL SPACES

— contents —

LIVING BIG IN A TINY HOME

THE A TO Z GUIDE TO TINY HOUSES

Big Reasons to Go Tiny

With so many advantages, it's no small wonder so many people are choosing a pocket-size place to call home.

Tiny homes are having a moment—and for good reason. Small houses serve up big appeal on nearly every front. Lower building costs, less maintenance, cheaper utility bills and all around fewer possessions to manage are just some of the reasons people are flocking to the idea of scaling down their living spaces. The move to a smaller footprint can help us tread more lightly on the planet, put less strain on our finances and unburden some of the chaos and clutter of modern life. Giving up square footage even has the potential to add more personal time to a day. After all, you can spend that hour it would have taken you to vacuum a two-story home curling up with a favorite book instead. What's more, going small can help us reconnect with those we love. Couples and families who downsize find they inevitably spend more time together when there aren't large expanses of the house in which to escape.

What began a few decades ago as a quirky fad among a few brave souls looking to embrace small quarters is now a full-fledged modern movement.

The term "tiny house" has become as common in interior design and architecture circles as "Tudor," "split-level" or "duplex." With that popularity has come a surge in style and substance. Tiny homes are no longer makeshift, mobile abodes, but finely crafted creations that reflect the homeowners' priorities and aesthetics. (Although there are still plenty of options on wheels, too!) From quaint cottages to mini farmhouses and floating homes, these tiny houses are small, yes, but far from one-size-fits-all when it comes to design.

Of course, it can be an adjustment to reduce your space and your lifestyle, so consider *The Tiny Book of Tiny Homes* to be your primer for all things in pint-size living. This compendium of tips and tactics will walk you through the ins and outs of tiny-home ownership. All-in-one bathrooms? Kitchen storage? Zoning ordinances? All the head-scratching aspects of tiny homes are addressed in these pages. Read on to begin your journey toward living your best life in a smaller space. After all, it's true what they say: Less really is more!

—*Caroline McKenzie*

Living Big
in a
Tiny Home

Take a tour of some of our favorite micro houses, where innovative design, charming decor and stylish aesthetics offer maximum appeal.

165 SQUARE FEET

Giant Journey

A 25,000-mile excursion balanced a sense of adventure with a love of home.

Blogger Jenna Spesard spent one year traveling through the U.S. and Canada with her 165-square-foot tiny house in tow. She covered 25,000 miles, traveling below sea level in Death Valley National Park, over the Rocky Mountains and even through the ocean when her home was loaded onto a ferry. However, she notes, traveling with a tiny house is not a cheap lifestyle.

Unlike RVs, tiny houses are built using 2x4 framing, insulation and cathedral ceilings. This type of construction is heavy, and therefore expensive to haul. Spesard towed her 10,100-pound home with a Ford F-250 truck, averaging about 9 mpg and spending $700 a month on gas. But for Spesard, it was worth it. "I feel a special connection to my tiny home, and that, to me, is priceless."

READY FOR A ROAD TRIP? INVEST IN A GOOD GPS NAVIGATION SYSTEM. EVEN IF YOU'RE A SEAT-OF-THE-PANTS EXPLORER, IT'S THERE IF YOU NEED IT.

ROLL WITH IT

The loft (top left) holds a queen-size bed with space for books. Rustic accents include reclaimed barn wood floors and antique fruit crates (above). A storage loft gets light through a wood-framed window (bottom left). The open road (below) offered plenty of adventure.

CHEER LEADER
Brimming with flower boxes and beveled cedar siding—painted in an upbeat exterior color—the happy South Carolina home beams with style.

320 SQUARE FEET

Learning From Scratch

A South Carolina couple builds a family-friendly tiny house with the help of the internet.

Moving to a 3-acre property in South Carolina let Chris Pate and his wife, Sheradan, establish a little secure cash flow. Although the acreage included a 2,000-square-foot house, the Pates decided to build a 320-foot-square house to live in on the property and rent out the larger home. To control expenses, the Pates planned to construct the tiny house themselves. The only catch: They had no experience. Although they made good use of the internet to learn techniques, they eventually brought in an electrician and plumber to make sure systems were installed correctly. "You can learn just about anything online," notes Chris, "but that doesn't mean it won't take you two weeks and 20 trips to the home improvement store."

LOFTS WITH LOW CEILINGS ADD LIVING AREA AND ARE LEGAL—BUT THEY TYPICALLY WON'T COUNT AS OFFICIAL "HABITABLE SPACE."

BUILT TO LAST
A pull-out drawer and hinged stair steps provide storage. A wooden bridge connects the two sleeping lofts. The kitchen counter is framed with 2x4s and topped with walnut butcher block.

377 SQUARE FEET

Culture Combo

A blend of quirky English charm and the adventurous spirit of the American West creates a one-of-a-kind getaway house in the U.K.

EXTENSIVE GARDENS AND NATIVE PLANTINGS OF FLOWERS AND ORNAMENTAL GRASSES ADD TO THE AURA OF A NOMADIC GETAWAY.

GLASS ACT
Adding a porch with glass walls to a curved-roof Romani wagon, or vardo, created a unique vacation spot in Cornwall, England.

CIRCLE THE WAGON

The unique curved roof arches over the main sitting room and kitchen. Reclaimed wood elements add a rustic touch to the bedroom and bathroom. A curbless glassed-in shower helps the bathroom feel larger.

Sarah Stanley spotted a whimsical wheeled hut and was immediately smitten with its rustic walls and curved, Romani wagon–style roof. As the director of Unique Homestays, a U.K. home rental service, she also knew that with some modifications, it could be turned into a unique vacation house. "The Romani wagon set the scene for an abode with a nomadic soul," she says. "We wanted its features to reflect that." She chose an American West theme for the 377-square-foot home, shown in everything from colorways to the handmade feel of the rugs and furnishings, while reclaimed materials take the edge off an addition to the back of the hut. "I love the fact that so many items here have a history," she explains. "They have an interesting patina that just can't be recreated."

411 SQUARE FEET

Cottage Classic

High-end materials (and a focus on details) define this New England oceanside retreat.

WINDOWS TO THE WORLD
To break up the roof's pitch, make the house appear bigger, and let in more natural light, architect Mac Lloyd included four dormers, two along each side of the roof of the home.

W hen Mac Lloyd—co-owner with his wife, Lucy, of Creative Cottages LLC—designed this Freeport, Maine, oceanside retreat for homeowner Beth Marcus, he had many parameters—lot size, eco-concerns and proximity to water, setbacks, building codes—and, of course, Beth's design goals. She wanted "something cozy." They delivered, with a 411-square-foot house that's a classic colonial-style home writ small. The cottage is basically a single large area that encompasses a full kitchen, elegant bathroom, living room with a fireplace, bedroom and loft, creating a sophisticated, light-filled home.

A NEUTRAL COLOR SCHEME, SUCH AS THE WHITE-AND-LIGHT-GRAY ONE USED HERE, OPENS UP SMALL SPACES AND LETS SOME DASHES OF COLOR REALLY STAND OUT.

WARM REGARDS

Radiant heating under the wood-grain ceramic tile flooring keeps the house toasty in winter. A wall of windows and glass doors offer big views and floods the bedroom and sitting area with lots of light. The kitchen is fully fitted out with a Sub-Zero under-cabinet refrigerator, a two-burner Viking stove, a 16-inch dishwasher and a combination pantry and broom closet.

456 SQUARE FEET

The Getaway

A Floridian follows her family tradition of heading to the woods of North Carolina for peace and quiet.

ABOVE DECK
Homeowner Alexis Waller surrounded her North Carolina cottage with over 400 square feet of decking.

A SHED-STYLE ROOF SLOPES IN ONE DIRECTION. ITS SIMPLE CONSTRUCTION MINIMIZED BUILDING COSTS WHILE MAXIMIZING INTERIOR VOLUME.

MOUNTAIN HIGHS

Canopies provide shade to the large deck. White walls and cabinets pair well with the wood elements. The master bedroom includes a king-size bed and opens out onto the deck. Transom windows add visual "space" to the house.

ashiers, North Carolina—population 200—is a pip of a town nestled in the Blue Ridge Mountains. Despite its diminutive size, the village and surrounding area are well-known for cascading waterfalls, peaceful lakes and a temperate climate. For Palm Beach, Florida, native Alexis Waller, summering there is a family tradition dating back to her great-grandparents.

During a tour of showcase homes, Alexis came across a small but stylish dwelling that completely captivated her. Offered by national homebuilder Clayton Homes, the 456-square-foot one-bedroom, one-bath cottage features soaring ceilings, plenty of windows and a modern-yet-rustic exterior. "I feel like I live in a tree house," she says. "I love that. It's a happy house with a great feeling!"

715 SQUARE FEET

Serenity at Eagle Point

Simple design and amazing views combine to create a tranquil haven in Washington state.

IN A SMALL HOUSE LIKE THIS, LITTLE LUXURIES—SUCH AS HIGHLY INSULATED, 8-INCH-THICK WALLS —ARE EASIER TO INCLUDE IN THE BUDGET.

To get to this Eagle Point, Washington, cabin, you walk a narrow, unpaved path that meanders through the woods. It's a calming stroll designed to help shed the hustle and bustle of everyday life. "The client is a very thoughtful, conscious person," notes Geoff Prentiss, designer of the cabin and principal at Prentiss Balance Wickline Architects in Seattle. In keeping with his client's predisposition toward restraint, Prentiss designed a rectangular, 715-square-foot, two-room house with a shed roof. A large expanse of divided-light windows frame the views from the inside, while outside, the house retains its purposeful austerity: There are no porches, decks or gazebos. "It's about engagement," says Prentiss. "When she steps outside, she's totally immersed in the surroundings."

AT EASE
A plant-filled shelf separates the living area and entry. The streamlined kitchen is sans upper cabinets. Reclaimed wood flooring adds warmth. Books are a soothing substitute for electronics.

21

WORLDS AWAY

Tucked into the rolling hills of New Hampshire, this cabin is made for relaxing escapes.

MONOLITHIC CONCRETE SLABS WORK AS BOTH A FOUNDATION AND TOUGH, STAIN-RESISTANT INTERIOR FLOORING.

743 SQUARE FEET

Way Outside the Box

A customized prefabricated cabin has its own unique character amid the natural landscape.

P eople hear the term "prefab home" and may picture a house that is devoid of character. You only have to look at the New Hampshire prefab house of Alex Grossman and David Park to dispel those notions. Built as a summer getaway, the 743-square-foot cabin features gorgeous timber-frame construction and exquisite details. Exposed beams, natural wood paneling and finely crafted hardware and fixtures bring this prefab house into the realm of architectural excellence. With its 14-foot ceiling, tucked-away loft bedrooms and tons of storage space, the open floor plan house lives large.

STYLE SMARTS
A 14-foot-high ceiling allows for a lofted sleeping space. The main bedroom is situated behind sliding barn doors. Both lofts have engineered-wood floors.

860 SQUARE FEET

The Bootstrappers

A pair of Seattle-based architects combine beauty with practicality in their eastern Washington getaway cabin.

AT ONE WITH NATURE
Beautiful vistas of the sweeping landscape make the small house feel absolutely grand.

Years ago, Mary and Ray Johnston, founding partners of their Seattle design firm, Johnston Architects, became enchanted with the sprawling mountains in the Methow Valley in Washington, and decided that one day they'd build a cabin there. But a new house just wasn't in the budget. "We really bootstrapped everything back then," says Ray. Eventually they pinched enough pennies to buy some land, where they camped out in a beat-up Airstream until they were ready to build. In that time, they got to really know the property and designed an 860-square-foot home in a cost-effective shape—a large rectangle with a nearly flat shed roof. Inside, a wall of floor-to-ceiling windows provides views to the valley they fell in love with.

THIS HOUSE IS ABOUT CONTRASTS: BETWEEN INTIMATE SPACES AND EXPANSIVE ONES, BETWEEN MATERIALS THAT ARE SLEEK AND ONES THAT ARE ROUGH.

ROOM WITH A VIEW
Wide eaves protect the generous front porch. The windows on the west side are 15 feet tall. The 8-foot-square bedroom can be closed off with a sliding door.

900 SQUARE FEET

Saving Face

A California designer with a passion for older homes restores the seaside mojo of a 1940s cottage in Laguna Beach.

675

SIMPLE DETAILS, SUCH AS DIVIDED-LIGHT WINDOWS AND FLOWER BOXES, HELP GIVE SMALL HOUSES PERSONALITY.

LOW PROFILE
A low fence with classic detailing is in keeping with the scale of the house.

C lark Collins had one word to sum up the little cottage he found for sale in Laguna Beach, California: "deplorable." Although the circa-1946 900-square-foot house had fallen into disrepair, Clark—who owns the design/build firm Collins Design & Development—saw it as a blank canvas that needed some TLC. He researched to find period fixtures, materials and details that matched the house's engaging personality. Old fiberboard paneling in the living room was replaced with tongue-and-groove board paneling. Worn carpeting was ripped up to reveal original oak-strip floors. Vintage light fixtures helped restore authenticity. "Not everyone wants to preserve older houses. But these are the types of homes that give a town its character," he notes.

EASY DOES IT
A bay window bump-out *ekes* out space in the galley kitchen. Simple woven blinds keep the focus on the view. The Dutch door and vaulted ceiling keep interiors fresh and airy.

The A to Z Guide

to Tiny Houses

From accessory dwelling units to zoning laws,
here's everything you need to know to make
the most of your scaled-down lifestyle.

ADU

Looking to add a tiny home as a guest cottage, work space or entertaining area to your property? Then accessory dwelling units—better known as ADUs—is a term you should become familiar with. This is the label for a separate second apartment or house that includes its own entrance, kitchen, bathroom and sleeping area. Unlike a tiny house parked on its own plot of land, an ADU shares the building lot of a larger main house. (Note: Depending on your municipality, ADUs may also be called accessory residential units.)

ON SOLID GROUND
Zoning regulations for ADUs vary widely from state to state, and often differ for tiny homes on wheels (opposite page, far left) versus those on a foundation.

B

BARN DOORS COME IN A VARIETY OF STYLES, INCLUDING GLASS, PANELED AND FLUSH AND CAN BE PAINTED OR LEFT UNFINISHED.

BARN DOORS

Barn doors—also known as sliding track doors or exposed pocket doors—are a tiny-home stalwart thanks to their minimal encroachment on floor space. Suspended from a track system, they slide on the outside of a wall, which means they don't take up any precious room when they open and close. Choose one with glass panels to help light flow between rooms, or a mirrored front to maximize available natural light and create the illusion of added space. Barn door hardware ranges from roughly $50 at a farm-supply shop to several hundred dollars from a designer retailer.

B

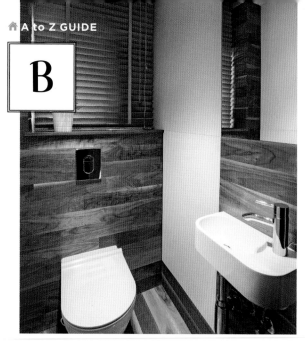

Mini-size fixtures made for half baths give you all the functionality of full-size versions. Mixing surface finishes (such as the tile and wood-panel bath, right) help a small space look and feel larger.

BATHROOMS

Trying to fit all the essential features into a super-small bathroom can feel like a clown car gag minus the laughter. But options are plentiful for a bathroom that cleans up nicely. Tankless water heaters provide hot water when you need it—and eliminate bulky holding tanks. There's also the option of an all-in-one bathroom, which is a single waterproofed space that has a sink faucet attached to a flexible pull-out supply tube that doubles as a showerhead (at right).

COMPACT VANITIES
INCLUDE A SINK, A
SINGLE-LEVER FAUCET,
A COUNTERTOP AND
STORAGE SPACE.

35

B

BUILDING CODES

Building codes have major impacts on how houses are built and occupied in this country. When it comes to tiny houses, the International Residential Code (IRC) should be used. The 2018 IRC Appendix Q: Tiny Houses, voted into law in 2016, is still essential for anyone interested in building a tiny house. It affords special provisions for common challenges found, such as ceiling heights, loft usage and access, room size and emergency egress. Those building a tiny-house RV should refer to the American National Standards Institute (ANSI) 119.5 and National Fire Protection Association (NFPA) 1192. These rules are more lenient than residential construction codes; however, the typical end result is a structure that is not classified as a primary residence.

DIY MASTERS
Many homeowners, like Erika and Tish Campbell, right, decide to build their own tiny homes, with the help of online and/or in-person workshops. The Campbells completed their project (shown here) in 18 months.

MODULAR DWELLINGS
GENERALLY FALL UNDER
LOCAL BUILDING CODE
REGULATIONS.

B

You don't always need a loft for your sleeping space.

•••
HIDDEN BEDS
ARE WIZARDS OF
FUNCTIONALITY
AND OFFER A SMART
SOLUTION FOR
SMALL SPACES.
•••

BUILT-IN BEDS

Whether a twin, queen or king, a bed is one of the largest—and most essential—items you'll need in your home. Enter built-in bed solutions that smartly integrate a sleeping space into the floor plan of the home. From a classic fold-down Murphy bed to bunk beds with strategic storage, the placement and functionality of your bed is worth sleeping on.

TUCKED IN
Fold-up beds are designed to be lifted and lowered with ease and feature all the comfort of a standard sleeper.

B

BUSES & VANS

Buses and vans are a burgeoning subcategory of the tiny-house movement. These oversize vehicles are being converted into ready-to-hit-the-road abodes complete with kitchens, bathrooms and bunk beds. They offer an easy-to-travel alternative to RV-style tiny houses, which require a trailer hitch and truck for toting. And even after being converted into living space, they typically clock in as far more affordable than most tiny homes. There's also the kitschy style factor of calling a retro school bus home.

●●●

CALLING A BUS OR VAN HOME MEANS IT IS EASY TO PARK FOR THE EVENING (OR A WEEK!) AT A CAMPGROUND OR RV PARK.

●●●

BE PREPARED
While not as pricey as building from scratch, there are costs associated with converting a bus or van into a more livable space, including flooring, insulation and ceiling materials.

C

MOBILE FURNITURE HELPS A SINGLE SPACE TRANSITION SEAMLESSLY BETWEEN MULTIPLE USES.

CASTERS

Flex space takes on new meaning in tiny homes, where a room's function may change by the hour. (Breakfast room to home office, anyone?) Enter casters, which can turn any piece of furniture into a mobile marvel. Both rigid (rolls in a straight line) and swivel (freely rotates nearly 360 degrees) styles allow homeowners to convert stationary items such as desks, islands and even sofas into portable elements of a room. In the home above, the vintage door-turned-coffee table features four oversized casters that let it be pushed out of the way when needed. Available at hardware stores for as little as $10, casters can be attached with a basic electric drill.

TURN HEADS

You can add casters to just about anything: Turn a kitchen caddy into a movable garden table, rework storage units or roll your bed out of sight.

43

C

DREAM BIG
If your child likes to doodle on walls, they'll love this chalkboard transformation, where they can let their imaginations run wild!

Some experts use cola to clean chalkboard paint off walls.

SALT & PEPPER

CHALKBOARD PAINT

This recent darling of the design world is especially well suited for tiny homes. The paint turns any surface into a hardworking chalkboard, giving dual purpose to your walls where you can write notes, reminders and sweet nothings. Fear not: The paint is available in numerous colors, not just run-of-the-mill black and green. Expect to pay about $15 for 8 ounces at your local crafts or home-improvement store, or online.

Shopping list

→ cheese
→ milk
→ bread
→ yoghurt
→ dipes
→ lemon
→ wine
→ banana
→ olive
→ tomato
→ champange

ADD A LAYER OF MAGNETIC PAINT
TO THE CHALKBOARD AND YOU CAN
DISPLAY PHOTOS OR OTHER OBJECTS.

VINTAGE CHARM
You can also use chalkboard
paint on furniture. The
ultra-matte finish gives off a
rustic, shabby-chic aesthetic.

C

STEP IT UP
Nestle a combo
washer/dryer unit
under a loft stairway.

COMPACT, MULTIUSE
APPLIANCES
PACK TONS OF
FUNCTIONALITY
INTO TIGHT QUARTERS.

Washer/dryer appliances can be tucked away under counters or vanities. Most are about 33 to 39 inches tall, 23 to 27 inches wide and 22 to 30 inches deep.

COMBO WASHER & DRYER

As the name implies, a combination washer and dryer, or all-in-one washer-dryer, contains a washing machine and a clothes dryer in a single unit approximately the size of a standard washing machine. The two-in-one appliance is a popular choice for tiny-home owners since it takes up half the space of a traditional washer and dryer. Additionally, many do not require an external air vent and some are designed to be portable so they attach to a sink instead of their own water line.

C

CONVERTIBLE COUNTERS

Don't be fooled! A kitchen countertop is anything but a fixed household item. Proper prebuilding planning—and a little ingenuity—can let this kitchen essential serve double functions, whether it folds out to provide a "dining table" or has an insert that lets you swap out appliances for more work space. The walnut countertop shown here has a section that allows the homeowner to cover the part of the countertop where a two-burner gas stove resides.

A walnut insert conveniently covers bulky burners.

IN A TINY HOUSE,
EVERY SQUARE FOOT
SHOULD HAVE A
SPECIFIC PURPOSE AND
AID FUNCTIONALITY.

D

BY THE BOOK
Declutter a reading nook (here and opposite page) by mounting bookshelves above doorways.

DOORWAYS

Doorways can be more than a pass-through from one space to another. That little section of wall above the door is all but begging to become a storage spot. Outfit the area with a shelf, or shelves, and use it as an overflow area for pantry items, shoes, cleaning supplies and more. This is also a nice place to hang decorative items or keepsakes when wall space is limited elsewhere.

> **VAULTED CEILINGS HELP A SMALL SPACE LOOK BIGGER—WITH THE ADDED BONUS OF GIVING YOU MORE OVERHEAD STORAGE.**

STACK 'EM UP
Modular cabinets can store items that you need but don't regularly use (such as holiday decorations) up and out of the way.

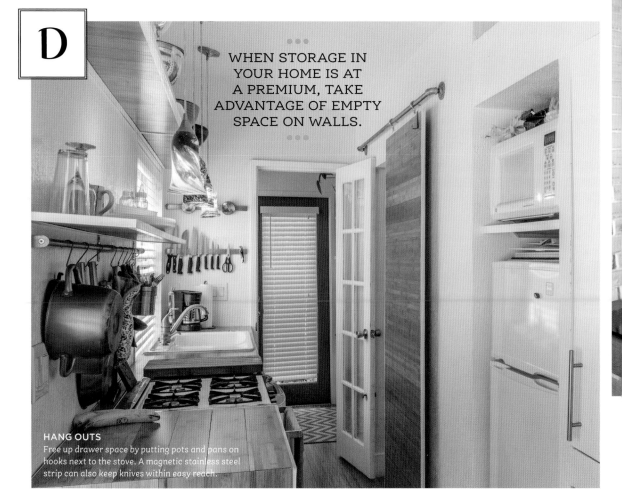

D

WHEN STORAGE IN
YOUR HOME IS AT
A PREMIUM, TAKE
ADVANTAGE OF EMPTY
SPACE ON WALLS.

HANG OUTS
Free up drawer space by putting pots and pans on
hooks next to the stove. A magnetic stainless steel
strip can also keep knives within easy reach.

HOOK IT UP
Take advantage of your kitchen's vertical space with rods and hooks that let you hang utensils and cutting boards right where you need them.

DOWELS & RODS

Maximizing vertical space is an imperative for small-space living. Dowels and rods let you take advantage of open wall space for minimal cost or effort. Available at crafts or hardware stores for less than $5, wooden dowels and metal rods can be attached to a kitchen wall for an easy-to-reach spot to hang utensils, pans, serving pieces and more. The storage is equally well suited for bathroom items.

GET CREATIVE
Use everyday storage items such as Mason jars as centerpieces for dinner parties.

DOWNSIZING

Scaling down to a tiny dwelling unit requires an evaluation of space and stuff. Start by making a list of the "essentials"—objects that are absolutely required for daily and weekly living, such as your bed or toothbrush. On the same front, are there items you once considered essential that you could live without? For example, a clothes-drying rack (like the one on the opposite page) could suffice in place of a space-zapping dryer appliance. With the essentials identified, consider what "nonessential" items you might have room for. These are objects that are not required but may add personal character, such as favorite books or family photos. Finally, pinpoint what "shared" items can be passed between family, friends and neighbors. For example, a set of eight place settings isn't needed every day but can be borrowed when there's a party.

WHEN YOU'RE SHORT
ON SPACE, THINK BIG IN
THE WAYS YOU CAN USE
HOUSEHOLD ITEMS.

MOVE IT
Foldable items, like
a drying rack, easily
stow away and can
even be used for
other purposes, like
drying herbs.

GOING GREEN
Lower building costs means you can splurge on eco-friendly specs such as Energy Star-certified lighting, fixtures and appliances.

ECO-FRIENDLY

It's no surprise that many tiny-home enthusiasts are also environmentalists at heart. Living in a tiny house can help you and your family dramatically reduce your carbon footprint. A 2019 study from Virginia Tech found that, on average, people who downsized into a tiny home reduced their energy consumption by 45%. Beyond direct energy usage, limiting household purchases, building with reclaimed or recycled materials and integrating features such as solar panels or composting toilets can all positively impact the planet, too.

BIG PAYOFFS
Design features like a green roof and solar panels can help drastically curb energy costs while reducing carbon footprints.

TINY HOUSES ONLY REQUIRE ABOUT SIX LIGHT BULBS, COMPARED TO 45 IN AN AVERAGE-SIZE HOME!

E

EXTERIORS

Just because it's tiny, doesn't mean it can't make a big statement! The outside of a tiny home presents the perfect opportunity to go all in with a favorite color, architecture style or even hobby. (Example: The outside of the 176-square-foot home shown here features a climbing wall.) Having a small canvas also makes it more economical to use higher-end materials such as brick, or a fiber-cement siding such as HardiePlank.

WHETHER IT MATCHES AN AESTHETIC OR A LIFESTYLE, THE EXTERIOR SETS THE TONE FOR YOUR HOME

BUILT-IN FUN
An outdoor-loving couple had a 12-foot-high, 24-foot-wide climbing wall built to give them some exercise while they traveled around.

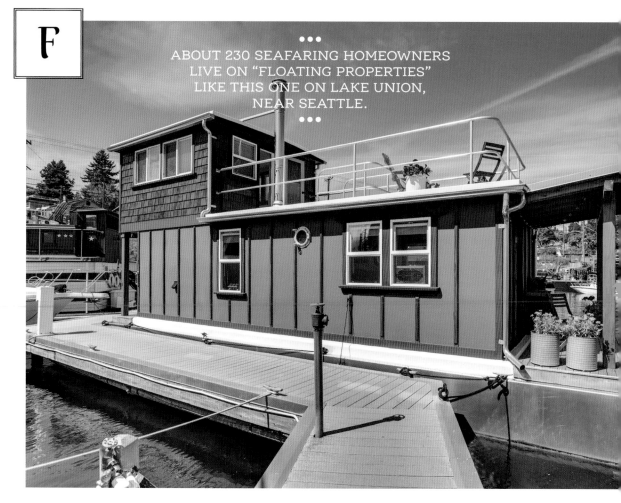

F

ABOUT 230 SEAFARING HOMEOWNERS
LIVE ON "FLOATING PROPERTIES"
LIKE THIS ONE ON LAKE UNION,
NEAR SEATTLE.

FLOATING HOUSES

Not all tiny homes are landlocked! Floating houses are an increasingly popular sect within the tiny-house movement. As its name implies, a floating house is a residential structure that sits on the water. Although these can be constructed at any size, most qualify as tiny homes. Different from a houseboat, a floating house is meant to be placed on a floating foundation and permanently connected to public utilities.

F

DOUBLE DUTY
Choose pieces that can serve multiple purposes, like this sleeper sofa.

FURNITURE

The most livable tiny homes are those brimming with features and amenities typically found in average-size houses. A mix of stylish and functional furniture can make the difference between a small home that feels deprived and one that is delightful. Foldable, freestanding pieces have the ability to go almost anywhere and stow easily when not in use. Hidden furniture—such as Murphy beds, fold-out tables and pop-out sofas—disappear into walls or behind cabinet doors so they only take up space temporarily.

Furniture can fold to fit into surprisingly small spaces!

63

G

GREEN PASTURES
A garden roof, packed with live succulents, grasses and wildflowers, can last up to 40 years.

GARDEN ROOF

Also known as a living roof, a garden on top of a home can be prohibitively expensive. But the smaller footprint of a tiny abode makes them a more viable option. They are typically created by covering the entire roof deck with an impermeable material such as PVC, polyethylene or EPDM sheeting. Edging is then attached to the roof's perimeter and the surface is lined with plastic trays containing lightweight soil and live plants. Succulents are among the preferred plants for garden roofs because they are good at retaining water in intense sunlight. Grasses, wildflowers and other native plants are also popular selections.

GARDEN ROOFS
ABSORB SOUND,
RELEASE OXYGEN AND
OFFER A HABITAT FOR
BUTTERFLIES AND
SONGBIRDS.

GRANNY PODS

This is a generic term for an accessory dwelling unit that's intended for an aging parent to live in close proximity to a caregiver. It's become increasingly popular for families who want to have older relatives staying nearby while still maintaining their independence. Although not a legal description, tiny homes can be designed specifically as "granny pods," with ergonomically friendly spaces, barrier-free bathrooms and generous lighting.

SAFE SPACE
Slip-resistant floors and
wide doorways help make
granny pods more accessible.

● ● ●
GRANNY PODS CAN
ALSO BE USED AS GUEST
SUITES, OFFICES AND
RENTAL PROPERTIES—
NO GRANNY REQUIRED!
● ● ●

H

GAS UP
A gas fireplace (right) or wood-burning stove (left) can add a bit of toasty comfort to a room without taking up much space.

HEATING & COOLING

Implementing smart heating and cooling systems begins as early as the building process. Insulating the walls and roof with a material such as spray foam will help a house regulate its temperature before heat or air conditioning are even installed. For warm weather, compact wall-mounted mini-split HVAC systems are ideal, because they don't need ductwork running in walls and floors, saving invaluable space. You can also use a small window air conditioner, since you won't have a lot of square footage to cool. On crisp days, a wood-burning stove will add both physical and visual warmth, or you can opt for electric wall heaters.

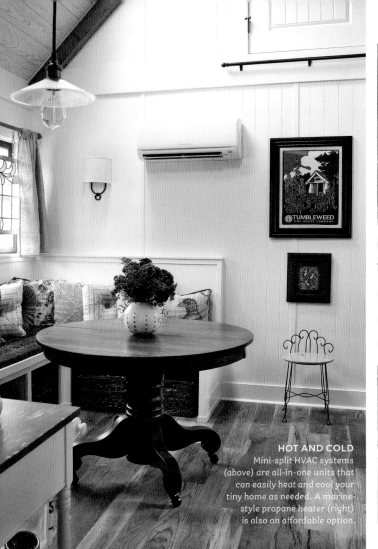

HOT AND COLD
Mini-split HVAC systems (above) are all-in-one units that can easily heat and cool your tiny home as needed. A marine-style propane heater (right) is also an affordable option.

1

ONE STUDY FOUND
INDOOR PLANTS
REDUCED THE
INCIDENCE OF
HEADACHES BY 24%.

INDOOR PLANTS

Bringing some of the outdoors in can help to liven up a house, add fresh pops of color and detoxify the air inside your home. Plants help improve indoor air quality thanks to their natural ability to turn carbon dioxide into oxygen, getting rid of specific airborne toxins that can cause allergies and respiratory distress. This is especially true in a tiny home, where the limited space means more impact per plant. Some varieties that are known for their purifying abilities include aloe, peace lily and mother-in-law's tongue.

GROWING TREND
Indoor plants can help remove harmful gases such as formaldehyde from the air—and can be used to make any space feel brighter and more alive.

J

WITH A LAPTOP AND AN
INTERNET CONNECTION,
IT'S EASIER THAN EVER
TO COMBINE WORK
AND TRAVEL.

MAKE ROOM
Having a dedicated work space will help you stay focused on the job at hand.

JOB OPPORTUNITIES

Tiny-home living may just help you do more than save money. It also has the potential to help you make money. How so? Owning a mobile tiny home means you can up and move your home anywhere work may take you. The expenses of moving to a new city for a career change become far less when you can skip the moving companies and real estate agents and simply hit the road with your house on board! With much of the world now working from home, mobile tiny-home living also means you can sate your wanderlust while simultaneously clocking in for your nine-to-five.

K

CLOSE QUARTERS
MEAN COMMUNICATION
IS KEY, ESPECIALLY
WHEN IT COMES
TO CO-PARENTING!

BOTTOM LINE

Living in a tiny
home cuts down
on expenses like
mortgages and
utilities—so you can
spend more of your
money on things your
family may need.

KIDS

Kids are small and so are tiny homes. That
doesn't always mean to the two are a natural
fit! But with the right planning and attention to
family members' needs it can be done. Veteran
tiny-house parents recommend scheduled "me
time" for each child, whether that's an hour alone
in their sleeping quarters or lounging solo in the
living room. Yes, conflicts are still sure to arise;
however, the close quarters often force resolution
and reconciliation more rapidly than would occur
for families who live in more sprawling abodes.

KITCHEN CABINETS

Some walk-in closets may be bigger than your small-scale kitchen! But no matter your layout— horseshoe, L-shape, galley or single-wall—you can work with limited square footage. What's the trick? Smart, think-outside-the-box cabinetry. If you find yourself limited by traditional modular cabinets with sizes that don't sync up with your available space, you can fill in openings with narrow pull-out shelving. DIY drawer kits that let you customize drawer widths are also an option; you can make drawer fronts to match the surrounding cabinetry.

SWING TIME
Drop-down cabinets in this home by Modern Tiny Living save space. Butcher-block counters can be sized to fit.

EVEN YOUR CABINETS CAN MULTITASK, LIKE THIS SPICE RACK THAT ALSO DOUBLES AS A SHELF.

OUT OF SIGHT
Kitchen cabinets are almost completely replaced by a storage wall and a spice rack above the sink. Panels slide open (inset) to reveal dinnerware.

L

MAKE YOUR MARK
Use fixtures to express your own style, whether that's boho chic or down-home country (like this rustic interior, complete with antler-accented chandeliers).

● ● ●

BOTH NATURAL
AND ARTIFICIAL
LIGHT HELP
SET THE MOOD
THROUGHOUT
YOUR HOME.

● ● ●

LIGHTING

Bright ideas abound for lighting your home. The right scheme will allow you to create various "zones" within a single space. For example, the area over the kitchen sink might offer bright task lighting, while a sitting area or dining table can feature dimmers that instantly add ambience. You can also up the style factor with unique decorative lighting in a pint-size space such as a bathroom. Look to sconces, both hardwired and plug-in, to free up valuable real estate from nightstands and desks.

LIGHT THIS WAY
Hanging fixtures (left and above) add both function and style. Consider the size and shape of the fixture, as well as the materials. Wall sconces (right) save space.

L

TAKING A STEP
A sturdy ladder is a crucial part of a loft design, but it doesn't have to be unsightly. A vaulted ceiling (inset) makes a loft bedroom feel more open.

LOFTS DON'T HAVE TO JUST BE FOR SLEEPING—YOU CAN ALSO CREATE A COZY STUDY SPACE.

LOFTS

If you've spent any time perusing photos of tiny houses, you've likely been charmed by a loft space or two. (Or 20!) Different from a proper second story, a loft is an elevated area in a room directly under the roof, usually accessed by a ladder. They are a common element of tiny houses, as they allow homeowners to creatively maximize vertical space, often resulting in larger kitchen and living spaces. Since they may have low head clearance, they are especially well suited for sleeping areas—a cocoon-like place to catch some z's.

OPEN UP
Good lighting and windows are important to help a loft feel airy, not claustrophobic.

M

Creative placements make small spaces look larger.

SHOW-AND-TELL

Frames can reflect a variety of styles, from boho to mod to country classic.

MIRRORS

Mirrors are more than a superfluous decorative flourish. (Or somewhere to check you don't have spinach in your teeth!) The design staple can also create a trick of the eye that makes a room or space appear bigger than it actually is. What's more, the reflective surfaces will exaggerate natural light and amplify surrounding views. From a strategically placed single mirror to a floor-to-ceiling assortment, the possibilities for integration are nearly endless.

ALL SHAPES

You can find mirrors in virtually any shape or size you want, with geometrics such as rectangles and ovals leading the way. Choose from framed or unframed versions, depending on the space and design aesthetic.

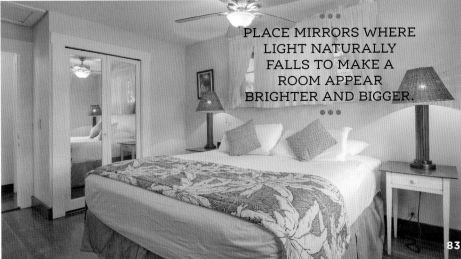

PLACE MIRRORS WHERE LIGHT NATURALLY FALLS TO MAKE A ROOM APPEAR BRIGHTER AND BIGGER.

M

FITTING IN
When space is at a premium, your sink can also double as a spot for food prep with a fitted cutting board. Store kitchen essentials in a drop-down cabinet.

MULTIPURPOSING

Can a knife double as a potato peeler? Will foil work as a dish scrubber? Does olive oil provide an alternate to furniture polish? Yes, yes and yes! Let your tiny-house journey spur creativity and inspire you to discover ways to reduce the quantity of items in your home by choosing objects with multiple functions. And it doesn't just have to be accessories: Look for furnishings that double as storage (a bed with pull-out drawers) or have multiple uses (a coffee table that also serves as seating).

IN TIGHT SPACES, IT PAYS TO BE CREATIVE. CONSIDER HOW TO MAXIMIZE EACH ITEM'S FUNCTION SO NOTHING IS WASTED!

A Murphy bed is hidden behind this shelf (see above right)!

TWO-TIMERS

When opened, this Murphy bed from ZeroSquared (above and left) reveals a large window. A bench seat (below) does double duty as a storage bin.

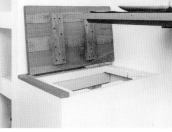

N

LOWER MONTHLY
COSTS, FRESHER
INDOOR AIR AND A
QUIETER INTERIOR
ARE ALL PART
OF A NET-ZERO
ENERGY HOME.

NET-ZERO ENERGY

A net-zero energy building is one where the total
amount of energy used by the building on an
annual basis is equal to the amount of renewable
energy created on the site. Due to their compact
size, net-zero energy is far more easily attainable
in a tiny home. Solar panels, high-efficiency
windows and insulation, and energy-efficient
HVAC, appliances and lighting can all help your
small home make a big reduction in its energy
usage—helping the planet and your wallet.

O

OPEN SHELVING

In kitchens, bathrooms, living rooms—and really just about anywhere—you can maximize a compact space by opting for open shelves over bulky cabinets. The streamlined storage will alleviate the awkward angles that can arise from squeezed-in cabinet doors. Bonus: The displays can transform utilitarian items into works of art.

USE BASKETS OR
COLORFUL BOXES
TO KEEP SHELVES TIDY
AND UNCLUTTERED.

O

●●●
STAYING
ORGANIZED
IS EASIER
WHEN
EVERYTHING
HAS A
DESIGNATED
PLACE TO GO.
●●●

ORGANIZATION

Organization is integral to happy tiny-house living. But it isn't a one-and-done accomplishment. Maintenance is critical to ongoing organization success. To ensure your small space stays in top form, implement weekly or monthly checklists where you tidy up and edit various areas of your house. For example, clean out the pantry the first Wednesday of each month for expired items. These simple practices will help you keep your storage systems shipshape and prevent clutter from taking over.

CUT THE CLUTTER
Spend just a few minutes each day making sure everything is put away in its place.

O

JUST BECAUSE YOUR LIVING SPACE IS ON THE SMALL SIDE DOESN'T MEAN YOU CAN'T ENJOY THE GREAT OUTDOORS!

ALL AGLOW
An outdoor firepit helps expand living space and creates a cozy spot for alfresco relaxing under the stars. Just make sure it's a safe distance away from your home.

GATHER ROUND
Many tiny-home communities
take advantage of common outdoor
space to bring people together.

OUTDOOR SPACES

Want more living space while still residing
in a tiny house? Look to the great outdoors!
Exterior extras such as firepits, grills, dining
tables, swinging beds and movie projectors are
just a few of the many ways that you can expand
your usable living space. Plus, the fresh air and
open scenery offer a new environment that can
help you recharge and embrace nature.

P

PAINT

For high style without any square footage at stake, look no further than a bucket of paint. The decorating cure-all can add personality to plain-Jane rooms and also help to define different zones within a small space. Plus, it's affordable and easy to change out over time. In this Portland, Oregon, tiny home, a cobalt blue paint job on the kitchen cabinets gives the house a hip boho-cool look—no space required!

●●●

A PUNCH OF FUN COLOR USED AS AN ACCENT CAN ELEVATE THE LOOK AND FEEL OF A SMALL SPACE.

●●●

Keep the hardware
simple when bold
colors are the focus.

P

ANIMAL HOUSE
Sacrificing small areas of indoor space for your pet's needs is essential to creating a harmonious household.

PETS

Small spaces can stress four-legged friends, but that doesn't mean your dogs and cats can't find domestic tranquility in a tiny house. Consider design elements that will help your pets engage in their daily activities with ease. For example, wall-mounted walkways invite cats to explore and get playful exercise. Pull-out drawers are a great way to store dog toys within easy reach and keep food bowls hidden away when not in use. Since living with a pet in a downsized space can lead to big messes, some pet owners set up outdoor cleaning stations to wipe paws before reentering. Watch your pets for signs of distress as you transition to a tiny home, and consult your vet should any arise.

HELP PETS WORK OFF
EXCESS ENERGY AND
STAY HEALTHY BY
GIVING THEM PLENTY
OF EXERCISE.

P

TRIAL BASIS
Those looking to try
on tiny-home living
for size can lease
a house in a rental
pocket community.

IF YOU ENJOY A SENSE
OF CAMARADERIE
AND MAXIMIZING
YOUR RESOURCES,
THIS WAY OF LIFE
MAY BE FOR YOU.

POCKET COMMUNITIES

A pocket community is loosely defined as a cluster of homes arranged on lots with shared common spaces. They are becoming increasingly popular among tiny-home enthusiasts, helping to foster a sense of camaraderie that many people find missing from modern life. Plus, with shared resources, they allow homeowners to maximize outdoor options such as gardens, firepits and picnic tables with relatively low buy-in and maintenance costs. You can even find pocket neighborhoods with pools, fitness centers, retail shops and other important amenities.

P

PREFAB

Prefab homes are one option for mini house construction. Prefab is a generic term for any house or structure that's built in a factory and then assembled at the home's site. (This type is different from manufactured homes that are completely built in a factory with no assembly on-site.) Both modular and panel-built homes are considered to be prefab. All prefabricated houses must meet local and federal building codes and pass regular inspections, just like any conventionally built house.

GOING FAST
A prefab model can be constructed on-site in as few as three months.

● ● ●

PREFAB HOMES ARE UP
TO 25% LESS EXPENSIVE
THAN TRADITIONALLY
BUILT MODELS.

● ● ●

HAVING DEDICATED FAMILY TIME, EVEN IF IT'S JUST FOR A SHORT WHILE, CAN BRING EVERYONE TOGETHER.

QUALITY TIME

Unlike the larger homes most people are used to, teeny homes provide little in the way of bedrooms and living spaces. That limited square footage translates into more time together for couples and families. Since retreating to their own spaces isn't an option, tiny-home residents enjoy increased time with loved ones. Most report that this togetherness fosters closer connections and better conflict-resolution skills, to boot!

R

STRAIGHT AND NARROW
Ranges can be found as narrow as 20 to 24 inches wide to squeeze into tight spaces (left). A cooktop (below) forgoes the need for an oven altogether.

RANGES & STOVES

As with so many aspects of micro home living, deciding on a kitchen range requires a bit of self-reflection. Being honest about what you really need will help you make better decisions about what will work best for you and your family.

Avid cooks may want to opt for a compact but luxe gas cooker. (Vintage electric stoves are also a diminutive and affordable option.) Homeowners who cook relatively infrequently may be able to get by with a basic, simple, induction flush-mount cooktop.

WHETHER YOU WANT SOMETHING THAT LOOKS RETRO OR TOTALLY MODERN, THERE ARE OPTIONS TO SUIT YOUR STYLE.

RECLAIMED MATERIALS

What's not to love about salvaged materials? First and foremost, incorporating them into your home is good for the environment, since you're using items already out there rather than incorporating made-from-scratch goods, and saving materials from going to a landfill. They're also usually easier on your wallet because you're getting them secondhand. Last but not least, they add unique style to a space, layering pretty patina and one-of-a-kind texture into a space. Given the small footprint of this category of homes, it is often possible to exclusively use reclaimed materials. Larger properties, which require more of everything, often fall short of that goal.

FLOOR IT
The wooden floors in this 362-square-foot cabin were salvaged from a 1927 home, then stripped, sanded, stained and refinished.

R

REFRIGERATORS

You can find fantastic models for your diminutive kitchen that are far more functional and stylish. Appliance manufacturers are now offering numerous options a mere 24 inches wide, with storage of up to 12 cubic feet. (For reference, a standard fridge has a 22- to 30-cubic-foot capacity.)

Under-counter refrigerator drawers can also glide to the rescue. No matter the size of fridge, decide before buying if you want your home to be completely off the grid. If the answer is yes, you may want to consider a propane refrigerator, which will keep food cool without requiring electricity or solar energy.

LET YOUR FRIDGE
BECOME PART OF THE
DECOR, CHOOSING ONE
IN A VIBRANT COLOR
THAT COMPLEMENTS
YOUR HOME'S STYLE.

BIG SURPRISE
Many of today's
refrigerators come
with a variety
of features and
extras, even in the
smallest models on
the market.

BE CONNECTED
Invest in having high-speed Wi-Fi for your property, a key amenity for many tenants whether they are short- or long-term renters.

●●●
CHECK LOCAL ZONING ORDINANCES AND BUILDING CODES TO MAKE SURE YOUR PROPERTY QUALIFIES AS A RENTAL.
●●●

RENTALS

Here's a new term for you: tiny income property. With micro houses a popular category on online vacation-rental sites such as Airbnb and HomeAway, many entrepreneurs are investing in tiny homes for supplemental income. In addition to the market demand for pint-size vacation properties, they are also a cheaper investment than a standard rental. What's more, less space equals less post-guest cleanup and maintenance.

S

TWO ON TOP
Twin skylights ensure a loft in this home by Modern Tiny Living gets plenty of daylight (and moonlight)!

SKYLIGHTS

Skylights increase the natural light available, helping a small space feel more open and inviting. If you opt for a style that can also be opened, it will come with the added bonus of providing ventilation. Depending on your climate, a skylight can also help to heat your home. Since some skylights are prone to leaking, this is one area of tiny-house construction where you may want to consider investing in a top-of-the-line product from the start.

Light flows in from above and all around in this bathroom.

S

LOCK AND LOAD
You can transform a living space into a dining nook with a few simple clicks.

A SMALL LIVING AREA CAN HAVE MULTIPLE FUNCTIONS WHEN FURNITURE MOVES AROUND EASILY.

Vary the height of a table depending on the purpose.

SOCKET STANDS

Originally used for boat manufacturing, socket stands bring lots of versatility to spaces throughout a tiny home. They feature a push-in and lock design that allows different pieces of furniture to mount to the floor as needed, and then move around depending on your preferences. The living room of this Washington, D.C.–area house, for example, has socket stands that turn a wooden top into either a desk or a coffee table. You are only limited by your imagination!

S

USING ENERGY-EFFICIENT APPLIANCES WILL REDUCE THE AMOUNT OF SOLAR POWER YOU WILL NEED IN YOUR HOME.

UP FRONT
Place panels where they will get the most exposure to light.

SOLAR ENERGY

Solar power panels collect energy from the sun and convert it into thermal or electrical energy. It's the cleanest and most abundant energy source in the world, and it's a popular choice among tiny-home owners who have a goal of reducing their global footprint (and their utility bills!). Before installing solar panels, you will need to consider how much energy your home will require. Factors to take into account include the size of your house, the number of occupants and the type of electrical items you'll need to run on a daily basis. The Department of Energy's online Appliance Energy Calculator can help you determine the energy used by various appliances.

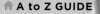
T

MICRO MATTERS
Composting toilets like these separate liquids from solids and use aerobic bacteria to break down waste.

TOILETS

When it comes to this unglamorous but essential bathroom fixture, there are four main categories to consider. Traditional tank toilets must be hooked up to plumbing in order to function. RV toilets look much like standard toilets, but are emptied through a hose that runs out of the side of the structure. Composting toilets dispose of waste through decomposition, much as material decays in a compost pile. Incinerating toilets burn contents off, so the bowl doesn't need to be rinsed with water. Check your local regulations to make sure you are in compliance with any restrictions before installing your indoor throne.

SIZE, COST AND STRUCTURE ARE ALL KEY CONSIDERATIONS IN SELECTING THE RIGHT COMMODE FOR YOU.

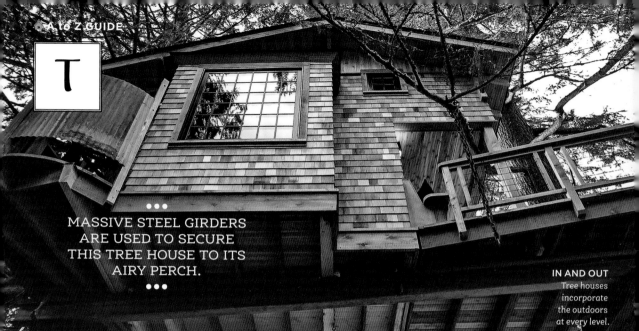

T

MASSIVE STEEL GIRDERS ARE USED TO SECURE THIS TREE HOUSE TO ITS AIRY PERCH.

IN AND OUT
Tree houses incorporate the outdoors at every level.

TREE HOUSES

Every teensy home has an element of magic to it. But the recent tree house tiny-home trend quite literally takes it to the next level. Companies such as Nelson Treehouse & Supply in Washington state, which built the properties on this page and near right, are constructing fully habitable homes with kitchens, bathrooms, heating and air conditioning nestled amid tree branches. The structures can last as long as the trees, which is why most are built in long-living species such as Douglas firs, cedars and oaks.

FINDING A HOME

Choosing the right location is critical in creating a safe, long-lasting structure. This airy retreat in Texas from Treehouse Utopia (below) was built amid large, sprawling trees.

U

PERFECT FIT
Clever drawer designs can store shoes, sports gear and more.

UNDER-THE-STAIRS STORAGE

When square footage is at a premium, think about any unused space, especially areas under staircases. With standard cabinet drawer hardware, many odd-shaped places can be transformed into pull-out storage units. Self-closing drawer slides help ensure invisible storage stays out of sight. And hinged stair treads can swing up to provide storage bins for spare linens and pillows, as well as for seasonal items such as boots, gloves and scarves.

PUT A STAIRCASE TO WORK AND TRANSFORM IT INTO A STORAGE UNIT WITH EASY-TO-ACCESS DRAWERS.

U

OPEN CONCEPT
Consider entry and exit
points when putting
in bathroom fixtures.

UNIVERSAL DESIGN

Universal design is a term coined by American architect Ronald Mace in the 1970s to describe design components that help to make a property or building accessible to everyone, including the elderly, children and people with a variety of disabilities. Elements of universal design include ample floor space for maneuvering, door and hallway clearance, ramps, handrails and grab bars. While some of these features may seem incompatible with tiny-house living, that's actually far from the case! Planning prior to construction will allow you to integrate any number of universal design elements—including the curbless shower shown here that allows for easy access.

A CURBLESS SHOWER MEANS ANYONE CAN WALK (OR ROLL) IN WITHOUT DIFFICULTY.

𝓋

VANITIES

Space-saving bathroom vanities are just as prized in a standard residence as they are a scaled-down home. Luckily, there are plenty of options on the market. Compact vanities include a sink, a single-lever faucet, a countertop and storage space. Floating storage keeps floor space clear, giving a room an airy, open feel. A classic example is a wall-mounted bathroom vanity that hides plumbing drains, while allowing access underneath the cabinet to clean the floor.

SIZE IT RIGHT
Choose vanity cabinets that are scaled down for small spaces.

FLOATING VANITIES GIVE YOU PLENTY OF ROOM TO CLEAN UP WHILE PROVIDING STORAGE FOR BATHROOM ITEMS.

v

EVEN IF YOU DON'T HAVE ROOM FOR A FULL CLOSET, YOU CAN EASILY ADD STORAGE SPACE TO WALLS.

VERTICAL SPACE

The square footage of your floor space might be modest, but do you have other surfaces that you can use? Yes indeed! Shelves running from floor to ceiling can work in any room. In a bedroom or entryway, lower shelves are ideal places to stow shoes, while upper shelves are perfect for folded items or storage boxes. Inexpensive cabinets are another great way to maximize wall space, no matter your budget.

HEADS UP
Placing natural elements such as plants higher up makes any space look a little larger.

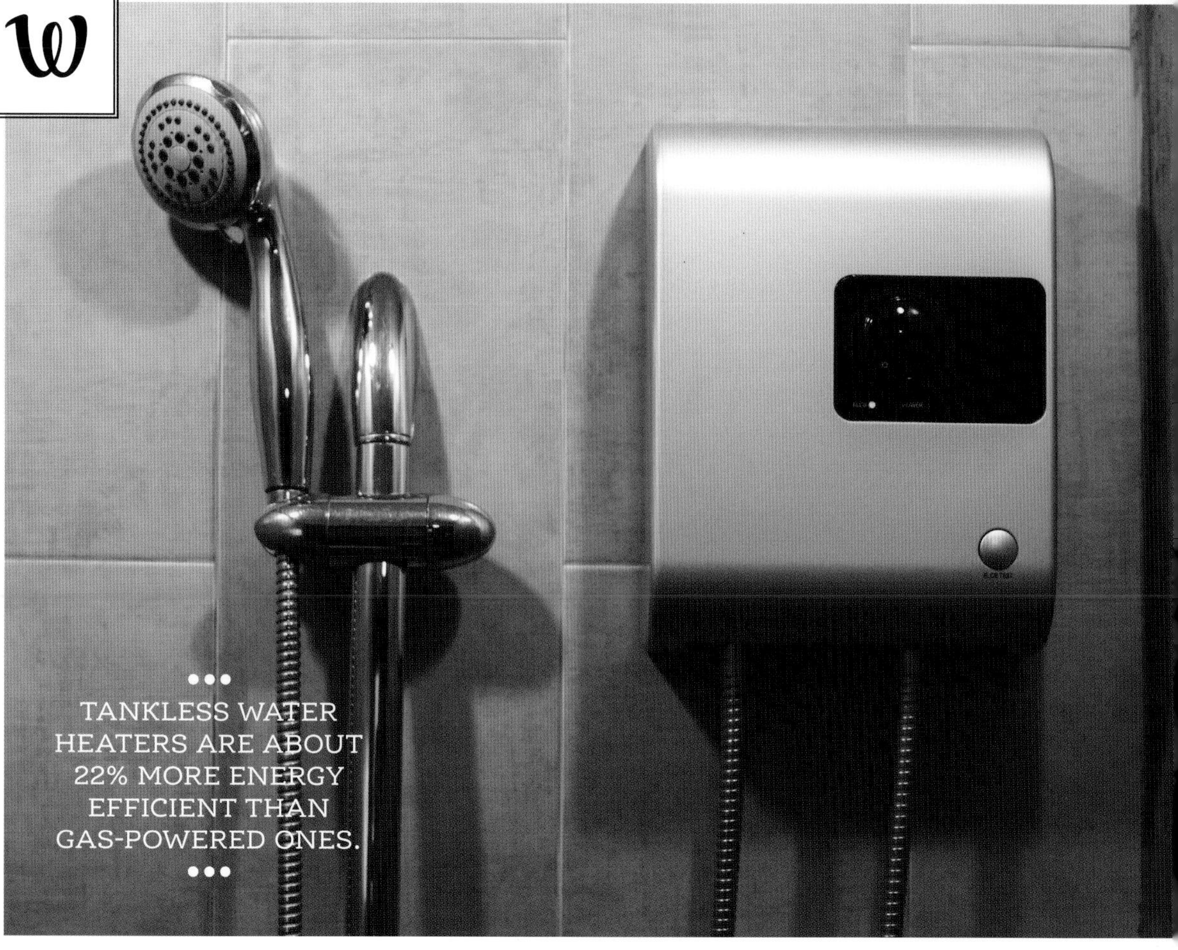

TANKLESS WATER
HEATERS ARE ABOUT
22% MORE ENERGY
EFFICIENT THAN
GAS-POWERED ONES.

WATER HEATERS

Bulky, traditional water heaters are the bane of many a tiny-home owner. (And plenty of large-home owners, too!) A tankless electric water heater uses thick copper rods to do the job, and is about a third smaller than a gas or propane one—not to mention quieter. Better still, this variety of tank heats water on demand (rather than constantly keeping water hot, even when you're not using it), making it an eco-friendly option. Heating water via solar panels is also a good green deal, although this style does require a large tank.

Tankless heaters provide hot water only when you need it.

CHECK IN
Confirm that your water system meets local building codes.

W

MORE FUN THAN AN
RV, A TINY HOUSE ON
WHEELS LETS YOU
HIT THE ROAD WITH
YOUR OWN STYLE.

EASY RIDER
*Make sure your tow
vehicle can handle
the size and weight
of your home before
you hit the road.*

WHEELS

Tiny houses on wheels, also called THOWs, are legally considered recreational vehicles or RVs. A THOW should be registered with your state as an RV and can't have more than 400 square feet of living space. If you're traveling with your THOW, you don't have to worry about residential zoning laws, but you'll need to find a place to park it. You can put it on the property of a friend or family member, or at an RV park. You may also place it on a property you own outright, but most states prohibit you from establishing a permanent residence in it.

X

CHANGE IT UP
Interior doors can match a room or have their own rough-hewn aesthetic.

X-BRACES

X-braces originated on barn doors, where they served the practical purpose of reinforcing the vertical boards to help the large doors hold up against high winds and other elements. Today, their appeal stretches beyond traditional barns and is a common design element, both structural and decorative, on cabinetry, headboards, storage bins and more. They often lend a modern farmhouse style in even scaled-down spaces and work well in different areas such as bedrooms, living rooms and entryways.

Y

• • •

THE ROUNDED WALLS
OF A YURT MEAN YOU'LL
NEED TO DO A BIT MORE
PLANNING ON WHERE
YOU'LL PUT THINGS.

• • •

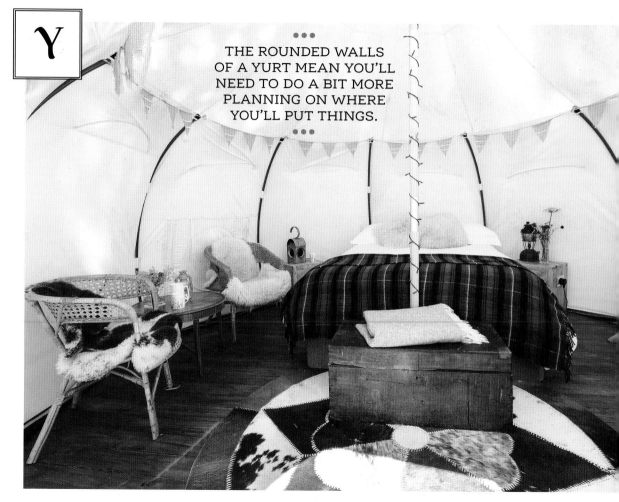

YURT

Yurts are ancient shelters that originated among nomadic groups in Central Asia. The distinct portable abodes feature a circular design, with fabric-covered accordion lattice walls and radial rafters leading up to a central ring. Today, numerous companies are offering ready-made yurts that can be installed by the buyers at a location of their choice—including places that are far off the grid.

Z

ZONING

Zoning ordinances outline where a house or structure may be placed. This subject gets quite tricky when it comes to micro homes. Many places in the United States don't allow you to build and live in a "tiny house" as the principal dwelling on a piece of land—although that is slowly changing, as the tiny-home grassroots movement pressures zoning boards to start thinking about accommodating smaller residences that help make housing more affordable. Zoning regulations are a big reason many tiny-home owners opt for a residence on wheels, which can offer more flexibility on placement.

REGULATIONS VARY GREATLY FROM CITY TO CITY, SO BE SURE TO CHECK GUIDELINES BEFORE YOU MAKE AN INVESTMENT.

SPECIAL THANKS TO CONTRIBUTING WRITER

John Riha

CREDITS

COVER Chris Pate **2-3** www.thebearwalk.com **4-5** Irvin Serrano; Mieke Zuiderweg; Johnston Architects **6-7** Woods Wheatcroft **8-9** Grey Crawford; Unique Homestays www.uniquehomestays.com; Irvin Serrano; Johnston Architects **10-11** Guillaume Dutilh **12-13** Chris Pate **14-15** Unique Homestays www.uniquehomestays.com **16-17** Irvin Serrano **18-19** Aaron Hogsed **20-21** Adam Michael Waldo **22-23** Jim Mauchly **24-25** Johnston Architects **26-27** Grey Crawford **28-29** Dmitry Galaganov/Shutterstock; rattiya lamrod/Shutterstock; agarangeusa.com; Brian Cole Photography; Minimotives.com; American Tiny House, LLC; salajean/Shutterstock **30-31** John R Rogers Photography; ppa/ Shutterstock; Courtesy Orlando Lakefront at College Park; John Riha **32-33** Steve Niedorf; John Riha; ppa/Shutterstock **34-35** Photographee.eu/Shutterstock; Mieke Zuiderweg; Dariusz Jarzabek/Shutterstock **36-37** John Riha (3); RESOLUTION: 4 ARCHITECTURE **38-39** Fotosearch/Getty Images; archigram/Getty Images; Jon Lovette/Getty Images **40-41** Victor Bordera / Stocksy United(3) **42-43** WorldWide/Shutterstock; v74/Shutterstock; orso bianco/Shutterstock; David Prince Images/Shutterstock; Baworn47/Shutterstock **44-45** olesiabilkei/Getty Images; kobeza/Shutterstock; Photographee.eu/Shutterstock **46-47** American Tiny House, LLC; Andriy Popov / Alamy Stock Photo; Zero Squared; Mireya Acierto/Getty Images **48-49** Paul Burk Photography (3) **50-51** GAP Interiors/Colin Poole; GAP Interiors/Jonathan Jones; GAP Interiors/Bieke Claessens; GAP Interiors/Julien Fernandez **52-53** Minimotives.com; Dmitry Galaganov/ Shutterstock **54-55** Westend61/Getty Images;New Africa/Shutterstock **56-57** Roger Wade Photography; ewg3D/Getty Images **58-59** Tom Baker **60-61** Photographed by: Virtuance www.virtuance.com; Harbor Cottage Houseboats (2) **62-63** Zero Squared(2); MK Lasek/Shutterstock; Resource Furniture **64-65** Woods Wheatcroft(2) **66-67** Dylan Jon Wade Cox for tinyhousesiesta.com; John Riha; Jamie Hooper/Shutterstock **68-69** Adam Michael Waldo; Roger Wade Photography; Nancy Nolan; Anice Hoachlander/Broadhurst Architects **70-71** rattiya lamrod/Shutterstock; Michaela Komi/Shutterstock; Alina Yudina/Shutterstock; Luoxi/Shutterstock **72-73** Mieke Zuiderweg(2) **74-75** Minimotives.com(4) **76-77** Modern Tiny Living(2); Mieke Zuiderweg **78-79** Roger Wade Photography; Jeremy Poland/Getty Images; Malia Schultheis, Interior Designer and Creative Director, Tru Form Tiny Photos Courtesy of Tru Form Tiny(3) **80-81** Roger Wade Photography(2); Tom Baker(2) **82-83** StudioBuell/New Frontier Tiny Homes; Ray Kachatorian/Getty Images; Oscar Wong/Getty Images; Brian Cole Photography; Kristin Hoshino **84-85** Laura Petrilla; Zero Squared(2); Laura Petrilla **86-87** Aliyev Alexei Sergeevich/Getty Images; adamkaz/Getty Images **88-89** John Riha; Will Austin/Johnston Architects **90-91** Jeremy Poland/Getty Images; Iglenas/Shutterstock **92-93** Aaron Kraft; River and Twine; Jeremy Poland/Getty Images; Mireya Acierto/Getty Images **94-95** Tom Baker(2) **96-97** Roy JAMES Shakespeare/Getty Images; Su Arslanoglu/ Getty Images; Jim Holden/Alamy **98-99** Courtesy of Ross Chapin Architects **100-101** Gregory Dean Photography(3) **102-103** Adam Michael Waldo; Free Road Films **104-105** agarangeusa.com; subzero-wolf.com; Marta and Tyler Anderson/@marta_anderson **106-107** Roger Wade(3) **108-109** GeorgeTsamakdas/Getty Images; Tik.tak/Shutterstock **110-111** Tony Anderson/Getty Images; Maskot/Getty Images **112-113** Modern Tiny Living; Dom Koric Photography **114-115** Malia Schultheis, Interior Designer and Creative Director, Tru Form Tiny Photos Courtesy of Tru Form Tiny; Paul Burk(2) **116-117** Ariel Celeste Photography/Shutterstock; salajean/Shutterstock **118-119** Sergey Ryzhov/Shutterstock; Katarzyna Bialasiewicz / Alamy Stock Photo **120-121** Nelson Treehouse and Supply (3); Treehouse Utopia, TX/www. treehouseutopia.com **122-123** Bilanol/Shutterstock(2); Upwind Studios **124-125** Martin Barraud/Getty Images; Adam Michael Waldo **126-127** ppa/Shutterstock; bmphotographer/Shutterstock **128-129** Richard Leo Johnson/Atlantic Archives, Inc./www.AtlanticArchives.com; CAST architecture; StudioBuell/New Frontier Tiny Homes **130-131** Volodymyr Shtun/ Getty Images; Santiparp Wattanaporn/Shutterstock; www.thebearwalk.com **132-133** inrainbows/Shutterstock **134-135** Harbor Cottage Houseboats; Kate Stoupas/Getty Images **136-137** GAP Interiors/Douglas Gibb; Mike Harrington/ Getty Images; GAP Interiors/Douglas Gibb **138-139** Jim West / Alamy Stock Photo(2) **BACK COVER** Johnston Architects

CENTENNIAL BOOKS

An Imprint of
Centennial Media, LLC
1111 Brickell Avenue, 10th Floor
Miami, FL 33131, U.S.A.

CENTENNIAL BOOKS is a trademark of Centennial Media, LLC

ISBN 978-1-955703-02-4

Distributed by
Simon & Schuster, Inc.
1230 Avenue of the Americas
New York, NY 10020, U.S.A.

For information about custom editions, special sales and premium and corporate purchases, please contact Centennial Media at contact@centennialmedia.com.

Manufactured in China

10 9 8 7 6 5 4 3 2 1

Publishers & Co-Founders Ben Harris, Sebastian Raatz
Editorial Director Annabel Vered
Creative Director Jessica Power
Executive Editor Janet Giovanelli
Design Director Martin Elfers
Features Editor Alyssa Shaffer
Deputy Editors Ron Kelly, Amy Miller Kravetz, Anne Marie O'Connor
Managing Editor Lisa Chambers
Senior Art Directors Lan Yin Bachelis, Pino Impastato
Art Directors Patrick Crowley, Alberto Diaz, Jaclyn Loney, Natali Suasnavas, Joseph Ulatowski
Copy/Production Patty Carroll, Angela Taormina
Senior Photo Editor Jenny Veiga
Photo Editor Antoinette Campana
Production Manager Paul Rodina
Production Assistants Tiana Schippa, Alyssa Swiderski
Editorial Assistants Michael Foster, Alexis Rotnicki
Sales & Marketing Jeremy Nurnberg